THE TORAH,
(*THE PRINCIPLE*)
OF GIVING

By Donald A. Peart

The Torah (The Principle of Giving) Copyright © 1998 Donald A. Peart

ISBN: 978-0-9852481-8-5

Cover Design by Jeshua Peart

Comments

- The New International Version and King James Version are the translations used in this book.
- The Author supplies the **bold** text in the bible references for emphasis.
- This edition was issued in September 2022.

Acknowledgments

"For it seemed good to the Holy Spirit..."

Table of Contents

Preface

In keeping with one of my concerns, I have kept this book as short as possible. Most of the youth of today and some adults do not have the patience or time to read extensive writings. This book is catered to their needs.

I have made it as succinct as possible. The queen of Sheba said, "Indeed not even half was told me," concerning Solomon's wisdom. In analogous manner, concerning the subject of giving, "not even half was told." This book can serve as a base to expand the readers' knowledge on the subject of giving. The book is very practical. It will also help the reluctant giver to give willingly. Yet, there are warnings for those who abuse this area in Christ's Church.

Saints of the living God should not be cursed, with respect to giving. This is the curse of the Law. The law mercilessly demands fulfillment. However, the Church is under the "changed" law of grace. This text is a guide for those who desire to be a giver in the right way. It will release the bondage from the curse of the law. Yet, the book will develop responsibility for giving. This text shows how **grace supersedes the law.**

Abuse of Charging

*1 Corinthians 9:18, KJV: What is my reward then? Verily that, when I preach the gospel, I may make the gospel of Christ **without charge**, that I **abuse not** my power in the gospel.*

One of the most abused areas in Christianity in area of giving and receiving is charging for the gospel of Christ. Paul, in this classic chapter on giving (1 Corinthians 9), gave an important aspect of giving and receiving that I believe some men of God may <u>intentionally</u> forget that the gospel of Christ is to be offered without charge placed on it. It seems that most meetings (conferences and/or seminars, etcetera) that ministers offer have a fee attached to it.

Paul, during his discourse on giving, asked a heart-searching question concerning giving and receiving. This is foremost for those <u>preaching</u> the gospel. He asks, "What is my reward then?" Listen to his answer: "Verily that, when I preach the gospel, I make the gospel of Christ **without charge.**" This is a heart-searching question, for the preachers of today.

When ministers preach the gospel, will they **do it "without charge?"** What if the people preached to do not give an offering, or the offering received is lower than expected; will the minister still preach to that same people again without anger?

In this generation, most would be angry or demand a certain offering. In fact, in this generation, believers have to pay a price to hear the gospel. Preaching has become a big business.

Contrarily, Paul says the gospel should be preached without charge. Then he gave the reason the gospel should be without charge. The apostle says, "That **I abuse** not my power (lit., authority) in the gospel."

When a man of God demands an offering from anyone, it is an abuse of "authority". When a fee is a prerequisite to attend seminar and conferences, this may be an abuse of authority. Remember, giving should be done **willingly** (2 Cor. 9:7). Therefore, when a man of God gets money by force, it is abuse. I reiterate if money is gotten by authoritative demand, it is **abuse.** Giving and receiving should be from a willing heart.

There are many in the world today who refuse to be a part of the church because of the violation of giving and receiving. Ironically, there are leaders who are not mindful that many in the world are offended by their abuse of this principle.

Some Church leaders may say people use this as an excuse for not serving God. These preachers are "blindly" right. The people's own words shall judge them. The people **not** being "saved" are what Paul was trying to prevent. Paul wanted to "save some." "I [Paul] have become all things to all men so that by **all possible means I might save some**" (1 Cor. 9:22, NIV).

Men of God "by all possible means" (which includes preaching without money being a catalyst) should preach the gospel to "save some." The aspiration for men of God should be for the world to be saved, by not abusing the principle of giving and receiving. They should be willing to preach without making money the reason for ministering.

1 Corinthians 9:19, KJV: *For though I be free from all men, yet have I made myself servant unto all, that I might gain the more.*

The aim of the gospel is not primarily to get offerings from God's people, or from those who come to a church fellowship. The men of God should focus on **gaining** people; the expectation is to **"gain the more"** believers for Jesus' kingdom.

We must make ourselves like a servant **for** those we are trying to gain for Christ. Listen to Paul's heart: "To the **weak** became I as weak, that I might **gain** the weak; I am made all things to all men that I might **by all means** save some" (1 Cor. 9:22). This is an area that the men of God in the church "must **master**".

The apostle says in 1 Corinthians 9:25, "And every man that strives for the **mastery** is **temperate** (lit; exercise strength) in all things". Paul then goes a little further: "But I keep under my body and bring it into subjection: lest that by any means, when I have preached to others, I myself should be a castaway" (1 Cor. 9:27).

Did you notice that in the context of **"when"** Paul made the statement above, he was discussing giving and receiving money? Men of God must **"exercise strength"** in this area. Do not become "a cast away" because of money.

The flesh must be kept under control. A man of God should not lose control of himself by demanding offerings and putting curses on people. The reward that a minister should receive after preaching the gospel is the reward of doing it for free, and/or not demanding a set fee.

Thus, Paul's statement does not negate giving to a preacher? The principle above brings the measure by which a man of God should walk in the process of giving and receiving. I did not say men of God should not receiving offerings at all. I am saying, "Preachers should not abuse people by authoritative demands for fees related to preaching the gospel." Preaching the gospel should be by **"necessity"** and not for money.

*1 Corinthians 9:16, KJV: For though I preach the gospel, I have nothing to glory of: for **necessity** is laid upon me; yes, woe is unto me, if I preach not the gospel!*

Here we see that "necessity" is laid upon those who preach the gospel. Necessity means constraint, as bending the arm up. The root word for this word is where we get our English word **"ache"** (Strong's #318, #303 and #43).

Preaching the gospel should be such a necessity to ministers, it should be an "ache" to them if they chose not to preach the gospel. Our motive should never be for gaining money,[1] but an **aching desire** to see people set free to dominate in their sphere of influence. This should be a **"good-ache,"** not a **"headache."**

In fact, Paul says, "Woe' is he if he did not preach the gospel for free. **With most men of God, it is "woe" for those who do not give them money.** Yet, listen to the result of preaching the gospel without being preoccupied with an offering, "For if I do this thing willingly, I have a reward" (1 Cor. 9:17a, KJV). The reward is the thing that was discussed above.

---

[1] 1 Peter 5:2

The reward is preaching the gospel without charging a fee (1 Cor. 9:18). However, there is another essential element for not preaching the gospel willingly, without a charge. The apostle states, "But if against my will, a **dispensation** of the gospel is committed unto me" (1 Cor. 9:17b, KJV).

This I believe is the most important reason the gospel should be preached to "whomever" without charge. "A dispensation of the gospel is committed" to everyone called of God to preach. Let me explain "dispensation" briefly.

Dispensation means **house law,** or **the law of the house.** This means that in every age there is a "law" of God's "house" (the Church) that must be dispensed to that generation. If the ministers of the gospel refuse to spread the house-law of the gospel or refuse to go to a particular Church to preach because the money is not big enough; then a law (message) for that people will be missing. Why?

The one, who is supposed to bring that particular message — house law — to those individuals, did not do it. Do you see it now? There is a law to every age concerning God's house. In this age and the age to come, the law of house is not only about the "common salvation," the house-law also concerns the "great salvation" and the "eternal salvation."

It is our duty as ministers to freely dispense this law of the gospel of the kingdom. "And this I do for the **gospel's sake,** that I might be partaker thereof with you" (1 Cor. 9:23, KJV). Wow! Did you hear the apostle's heart?

This should be the heart of all believers. We should become servants of all for the gospel's sake. It should not be done only for financial benefits. Paul also said that **false doctrine** is to "think that godliness is a means to financial gain" (1 Tim. 6:3; 5, NIV). In fact, the lust for fain has gotten so ridiculous that so called men of God put curses on people who do not give or tithe. They are teaching **half-truth**, as the reader will see later in this chapter. These are the Scriptures they use:

Malachi 3:8-9, KJV: *⁸Will a man rob God? Yet ye have robbed me. But ye say, wherein have we robbed thee? In tithes and offerings.* *⁹Ye are cursed with a curse: for ye have robbed me, even this whole nation.*

These are the Scriptures that preachers use to **curse** God's people. The sad part of this is that they are putting curses on God's people, and God does not agree with them. To really appreciate what I am saying, let us take a look at the text above in detail.

One of the most important words God states in the text above are the words **"this whole nation."** At the time God made this statement, he was talking to the **"whole nation."** The whole nation includes **people** and **priests** — as in preachers.

God was talking to the people, as well as the **"preaching priest."** The priests were guilty of abusing God's principle of giving, as well as the people. Therefore, when men of God are pointing one finger at the people, they have four pointing back towards them on the same hand.

The point is this: the priests were as much to blame as the people. With this in mind, let us see **how** the priests are guilty of robbing God. **Note:** I will also discuss another aspect of the priest robbing God in this book.

Malachi says, "Bring ye **all** the tithes into the storehouse" (Mal. 3:10). The word **"all"** is very meaningful. Jesus says, "Not the **smallest** letter, not the least stroke of the pen, will by any means disappear from the **law** until everything is accomplished" (Mat. 5:18). Therefore, the **small** word **"all"** is important.

"All" correctly means "whole" in the Hebrew text. The verse should read, bring your **whole** tithe into the storehouse. Now, "whole" have more defining applications than applying to **"all** the tithe" related to money or goods.

Whole also means, healthy, unhurt, restored, etcetera. The logical question is what was the **unhealthy** tithe the priests of that day and the preachers of today are bringing to God?

"O priests that **despise** my name. And you say wherein have we despised thy name" (Mal. 1:6, last part). The priests held God's name in contempt. That is, they were disrespecting God. They were abusing God by robbing Him of his whole **(healthy)** tithe and offering.

*Malachi 1:8, KJV: And if ye offer the **blind** for **sacrifice**, is it not evil? And if ye offer the **lame** and **sick,** is it not evil? **Offer** it now unto thy governor; will he be pleased with thee, or accept thy person? Says the Lord of hosts.*

This is a heavy statement made by God. He says it was the priests' duty to offer "whole," "healthy," "restored," and "unhurt" offerings to God. But they were bringing the **sick, lame, and blind** to God. What does this mean today? These offerings are symbolic of people.

*Romans 15:15-16, NIV: [15]I have written you quite boldly on some points, as if to remind you of them again, because of the grace God gave me [16]to be a minister of the Gentiles with the **priestly duty** of proclaiming the gospel of God, so that the **Gentiles** might become an **offering acceptable** to God, **sanctified by the Holy Spirit.***

Paul said it was his responsibility (priestly **duty)** to make sure the **"offering"** of the **Gentiles (people)** was **"acceptable."** He did not do it by himself. It was, and still is, the **Holy Spirit** who does the <u>sanctifying</u> as the priests (all ministers) preach the gospel. An important note in this verse, with respect to the subject of this book, is that **people** (Gentiles) are **"an offering."**

Paul also made it plain that the Gentiles (Ethnics) had to **"become** an offering **acceptable to God."** Therefore, if they were not ready to be offered being sanctified by the Holy Spirit, God would hold Paul responsible for neglecting his "priestly duty." Paul did make sure he did not offer lame and "sin sick" people to God. Paul did not ignore the Holy Spirit's working with him.

Preachers of this age are offering lame, sick and blind sheep to God. This means that there are people in some churches that are spiritually and/or naturally sick, blind, and lame; and the men of God are not allowing the Holy Spirit to heal the sickly. It is our duty to heal God's people with spiritual truths **through** the Holy Spirit. Are there hurt people in your church that were left unattended, **because they did not give the right amount?** If the answer is yes, go look to the flock of God.

Proverbs 27:23-24, NIV: [23]*Be sure you know the* **condition** *of your flocks, give careful attention to your herds;* [24] *for* **riches** *do not endure forever, and a crown is not secure for all generations*

Pastors should know the **"condition"** of the flock of God. They are not supposed to be "greedy for money, but eager to serve" (See 1 Pet. 5:1-4). The book of Proverb says, "Riches **do not** endure forever." However, the **"little flock"** will inherit the kingdom of God (Luke 12:32). It is your duty to allow the Holy Spirit to help heal all, restoring them to live in the great salvation. This is a spiritual truth.

Paul also says if people partake of spiritual things of others, then, it is the **duty** of the partaker to give carnal things (money) in return (Rom. 15:27). The problem is that some men of God want the sheep's money (carnal things). But they do not put in the hours, to hear spiritual things **(i.e., healthy words)** from the Spirit of God. They refuse to put the time in to be therapeutic to God's people. In other words, preachers are lazy in spiritual things for the flock, but assertive in money matters.

Listen to the Scripture: "You said also, Behold, what a **weariness** is it! And you have **snuffed** at it, says the Lord of hosts; and you brought that which was torn (robbed, stripped), and lame, and sick; thus, you brought an **offering**: should I accept this of your hands? Says the Lord" (Mal. 1:13).

To some, it is **weariness** to restore the flock. In verse 14a, God then pronounced a **curse** on the priests, for their apparent disrespect. "But **cursed** be the deceiver, who has in his flock a male (Jesus) and vow, and sacrifice unto the Lord a **corrupt** thing."

Jesus is the "male" in the middle of the church[2] who can heal us. However, the ministers would rather give a corrupt sacrifice to God. That is, ministers refuse to give the true principles of our Lord, who heals. Rather, they are lazy, saying it is a **"weariness"** to do it the right way, or "Holy Spirit way."

This maybe one of the reasons many people in God's Church are still sick (internally and physically), lame (physically and internally), and spiritually blind. The ministers refuse to pray intensely (Luke 22:44). Some have shut out the work of the Spirit, by saying the infilling of the Holy Spirit is an event of the past. Thus, they offer lame, blind, and the sick to God.

These sick people, time after time, are being offered to God with sick minds, lame walks, and blind hearts. What did God say? He refused the conditions

---

[2]Rev. 1:13, Rev 5:6

of these types of offerings. The blind (leaders) is leading the blind (followers) and they both fall into the ditch (Mat. 15:14).

My beloved if you are not being healed from the **sickness** of sin, then why do you give your **natural substance?** Find a man of God who is making you healthy naturally and spiritually to sow into. Do not sow into priests (preachers) whom God may have **"banned"** (Mal. 1:14). Some men are cursing God's people, but it is they who are **in danger** of being unapproved.

In the words of Paul, they might become **"cast away."** Malachi 1:14, the first part, says, "But **cursed (banned)** be the deceiver," the priest who knows better than offering sick people to God. **Jesus** offered to God the people He made whole. They were accepted in the beloved (Eph. 1:6, KJV). Jesus brought glory to God in making the "sin sick" people and the physically sick people whole again (John 5:31). Jesus made this plain to John's disciples.

"Then Jesus answering said unto them, Go your way and tell John what ye have seen and heard; how that the blind **sees,** the lame **walk,** the lepers are **cleansed,** the deaf **hear,** the dead are **raised, to the poor the gospel is preached"** (Luke 7:22, KJV). The people that Jesus offered to God were **accepted,** because He did not heal them partially (Contrast the false prophets in Jeremiah 6:14).

Jesus always made people "whole." Thus, He brought **glory to God** (John 11:4; John 9:1-3). Contrarily, the priests were **not** bringing glory to God by offering Him sick people. They were bringing Him **contempt or dislike** (Mal. 1:7). We must be opposite to this and follow in Jesus' footsteps. We as men of God must bring "whole" offerings to God.

God's repartee to the **nation** is to bring all (lit., whole) tithes into the storehouse. Thus, we see that the priests were included in this discourse. The priests were a part of the "nation." They were guilty of not bringing all, as well as, whole, healthy, unhurt, or restored people to God.

Yet, in spite of their lack of commitment to duty, some preachers of today demand the people's money. This should not be so. This is abuse, an irregular use of their position. As stated above, they call down imprecations on people by using Malachi. However, beloved, this thing is not supposed to be done to the Church.

The church is redeemed from the **curse of the law.** Men of God should not curse people for not tithing. Does this mean we do not tithe? The answer to that is absolutely not! The church **is** supposed to tithe, as we will see later. However, it is imperative that men of God do not curse people. Let us read Malachi again and compare it with another Scripture.

Now remember, I will be investigating **the abuse of men putting a "curse"** on God's people concerning giving and receiving. I will investigate tithing in a later chapter.

*Malachi 3:9, KJV: Ye are **cursed** with a curse: for ye have robbed me, even this whole nation.*

*Galatians 3:13, KJV: **Christ** hath **redeemed** us from the **curse** of the **law, being made a curse for us:** for it is written, **Cursed is every one that hangs on a tree***

Malachi teaches that the whole nation was **cursed** because they robbed God. We learn that this included the "preaching priests" too. Therefore, how can someone under a curse pronounce a curse? Most importantly, how can a preacher who is supposed to be of Christ, curse a believer who is also of Christ because of money? Do these preachers despise the grace of God? Do they not know the **heart** of Jesus?

Christ Jesus was "made a curse for us." He carried our sins on the **"tree" (cross).** Men of God ought to be more merciful with God's people, rather than cursing those that Christ bought with His blood. Jesus paid their price: the price of death by a cursed tree.

Therefore, men of God do not despise the grace of God, because if you observe the Law **to the letter** and not by the Spirit of grace, you are fallen from grace (Gal. 5:4-5). Let God worry about those who are cursed, or who are not cursed.

Because of the Spirit of Grace, tithes and giving are **received,** not demanded by pronouncing curses. Tithing as declared in Malachi **do** apply to the church, with the **exception** of the curse. How and Why? **"Christ redeemed** us from the **curse of the law,** being made a curse for us."

We are supposed to tithe. But, men of God, in the Church of the living Messiah, should not curse His corporate Christ. Moses did not make it to the promise land for hitting Christ twice. I warn through authority the Lord has given me, do not curse (hit) Christ twice.[3] You can die before you enter your promises.

Like **Melchizedek** who **blessed** Abraham, then Abraham tithed; so likewise, men of God should proclaim to the Church "God **bless** it! God **bless** it"

---

[3] God asked Moses to strike the rock the first time; however, Moses was to only speak to the elevated Rock the second time; and he did not do so

(Zec. 4:7, NIV)! The word of the Lord to Zerubbabel (a type of Jesus) who was rebuilding the temple[4] in Jerusalem was that Zerubbabel "will bring out the **cap stone** to **shouts** of ' God **bless** it! God **bless** it!'"(Zec. 4:7, NIV).

Capstone is feminine in gender in the Hebrew text. Therefore, the capstone in this verse is the Church. The Church is also called **living stones** (1 Pet. 2:5). Men of God who are helping to build the temple of Jesus should cry blessings, blessings, and blessings to God's people!

This is what Melchizedek, the true priest of God, did. He **blessed** Abraham **first.** Remember, there is a **change** of the priesthood. Therefore, there is a **change** of the **law** (Heb. 7:12). This new law tends to **endless life (eternal salvation),** not curses.

In conclusion, we understand that the servants of God must not abuse the gospel by demanding money. In the church I shepherd, I do not put any pressure on people to give. I do what I do, because I have a dispensation (house law) to give, by God's command.

Jesus said, "Freely you have received, freely give" (Mat 10:8b). Therefore, God will move on the heart of the people to willingly give. Yet, it is **their duty** to

---

[4] a type of the Church, see I Cor. 3:16

give (Rom. 15:27). I do realize that people forget their "duty" and need a little reminder. It is the duty of the Church to give to the man of God who is laboring lawfully on their behalf. That is, he is doing his best to walk with God in such a way that the people he affects will be healed. Men of God should not call down curses on God's people. Those who curse people do not know what spirit they are of (Luke 9: 54-56, KJV). But rather, they should gently encourage the church to give and tithe under the grace of giving. Do not major on the trivial things, forgetting the heavy matters: heavy matters like mercy, faith, justice, etcetera.

May our determination be to save the lost, rather than to drive them away! God is watching everything we do to, and for His sheep whether good or evil. Remember do not abuse the authority of God. Authority is given for building up, not destruction (2 Cor. 13:10; 1 Cor. 9:12). Authority is not supposed to be used to demand giving or tithing. Authority is meant to encourage the believer to tithe and give. It is better to receive than to take by force or manipulation. This is the principle that Melchizedek and Abraham exemplified.

Melchizedek Principle

*Hebrews 7:1, KJV: For this **Melchizedek,** king of Salem, priest of the "Highest" God, who met Abraham returning from the slaughter of the kings, **and blessed him [Abraham]**;*

Melchizedek[5] is one of the mysteries of the Bible. Abraham was privilege to meet this mystery priest. The Church of the Lord Jesus Christ is also favored to know about this man. But there is only one thing required. One must not be "dull (lit., lazy) of hearing." Once the church knows the mystery concerning this man, the church must not be **lazy** in doing what is heard.

Concerning Melchizedek, the book of Hebrews says, "Of whom we have many things to say, and **hard to be uttered,** seeing ye are dull of hearing" (Heb. 5:11, KJV). The phrase "hard to be uttered" means, in the Greek, difficult to be interpreted or translated.

Therefore, there are some things concerning Melchizedek that are difficult to understand. One of these mysteries is concerning his death. His departure can be explained from Scriptures. However, I will not do this at this time, seeing it might be difficult to receive. Yet more importantly,

---

[5] You may also reference my book "Melchizedek" for additional exegesis

discussing that mystery[6] would delay the topic at hand. The design of this chapter is to show the reader Melchizedek in the light of tithing.

*Hebrews 7:4, KJV: Now consider how **great** this man was, unto whom even the patriot Abraham **gave** the **tenth** of the spoils.*

This verse tells us Melchizedek was very great. He was so great Abraham gave "a tenth part of all" (Heb. 7:2). However, before I discuss the tenth or tithe, let me take a look at why Melchizedek is great.

*Hebrews 7:3, KJV: Without father, without mother, without descent, having neither beginning of days, nor end of life; but **made like unto the Son of God;** abides a priest continually.*

This verse is interesting. Among the words of interest is, he is made like the Son of God, and he remains a priest continually. To be made like the Son of God is the highest honor a person can receive. This fact was not haphazardly stated. He was made like the Son of God because he is a type of Christ's priesthood.

The time, at which Melchizedek met Abraham, he gave Abraham bread and wine (Gen. 14:18). The bread is the body of Jesus; and the wine is the blood of Jesus. Therefore, he gave Abraham life, which

---

[6] Please refer to my book Melchizedek

helped him to conceive Isaac. Jesus did the same. His body and blood are the life of the church (1 Cor. 11:27-30). We eat this body (bread) and blood (wine) at communion.

Melchizedek is also a priest of the "Highest" God. Again, it follows that Jesus is "a priest for ever after the order of Melchizedek" (Heb. 7:17). However, this priesthood is not like the priesthood of Aaron. The priesthood of Aaron **took** tithe of the people. But the priesthood of Jesus (Melchizedek) **receives** tithes without forcing people to give. **Taking** is different from **receiving from a willing offeror,** as the reader will now comprehend.

*Hebrews 7:5, KJV: And verily they that are of the sons of Levi, who receive the office of the priesthood, have a commandment to **take** tithe of the people according to the law, that is, of their brethren though they come out of the loins of Abraham:*

We see here that the Levites **"take"** tithe from the people. This was done according to **the law's merciless demands (though temporary).** The principle is this: the law takes from people forcefully. The law demands its fulfillment without mercy. The same is enforced by some in the Church today.

Some ministers are forcing[7] people to tithe. They are smiting God's people with curses if the people do not tithe. As indicated earlier, ministers are not supposed to use force on Christ twice. Moses smote the Rock "twice," and "that rock was Christ" (1 Cor. 10:4).

The first "Rock" Moses hit was a rock on the ground (Ex. 17:5-6). This is symbolic of Christ being smitten once (i.e., His death). However, when Moses got angry with the people, he smote a rock again. He was supposed to "speak" to the second Rock (Num. 20:8-12). The Hebrew word for the second Rock that Moses smote means **elevated rock.**

Jesus is now elevated never to be smitten again. The Church is also elevated in Christ (Eph. 2:6); and the Church is the "corporate Christ." Now the reader can understand why God was so strict with Moses concerning this issue. Moses hit Christ (the Rock) twice. This is like crucifying Jesus twice. Christ is also a corporate being.

The Scripture teaches that all Believers who are united as one body are Christ (1 Cor. 12:12). **We (the whole Church)** become Christ by baptism in the Holy Spirit (1 Cor. 12:13). Therefore, every time a minister smites God's people with curses, he is

---

[7] Under Jesus' Melchizedek priesthood, tithing is supposed to be done without being asked upon a person experiencing the Lord

smiting Christ a second time with the curse of hanging on a tree.

Now the reader can understand why God did not allow Moses to enter the Promised Land after he smote the Rock the second time. In light of the New Testament, it was like cursing Christ again. As stated in the end of the last chapter, sad to say, it is the same fate for those who smite the living stones (1 Pet. 2:5; Rev. 18: 20-21). Some ministers have become the **"school" bully.** The Scripture said the **law** was a **"schoolmaster** to bring us unto Christ" (Gal. 3:24). Christ came and freed us from the "schoolmaster." Yet there are school bullies (those who use the law to curse) pushing around the unlearned believers.

Modern day Pharisees use the curse of the Law as their fist (Gal. 3:24; Mal. 3:9). They are using the law (curses) to snatch (take) tithes from the people. Brothers and sisters, these things are not supposed to be.

They are doing what some of the priests did. They are taking tithe by the force (1 Samuel 2:12-17). Some use Malachi 3:9 as their motive. But they forget Galatians 3:13-14. The Melchizedek order is opposite. They **receive** tithe as the people give willingly as Abraham and Jacob exemplified in giving willingly. . They do not demand it. Why?

"For the **priesthood** being **changed,** there is made of **necessity** a change **also** of the **law"** (Heb. 7:12, KJV).

It is a **"necessity"** that the Church of the Lord Jesus Christ realizes that *the law is changed.* There is a new law. A part of this law states that the priesthood (ministers) of Jesus must **receive** tithes of willing givers, not take it by force from the people of God. The priesthood is changed. We no longer are under the curse of the law. We are under the blessings of His grace. The Melchizedek priesthood receives tithes. They do not demand tithes.

Hebrews 7:6, KJV: But he [Melchizedek] whose descent is not counted from them received tithes of Abraham and blessed him that had the promises.

In this verse we see the proof that Melchizedek **"received"** tithe from Abraham. With this in mind, I want you to note that Melchizedek blessed Abraham first, before he tithed. He did not curse Abraham first, like most men of God do today. This principle happened before the law, and the book proves this (Gal. 3:16-18). Thus, we who are of the promise should follow Jesus, our High Priest, who is made after the order of Melchizedek (Heb. 7:14-17).

In Genesis 14:19 Melchizedek blessed Abraham: "and he **blessed** Abram, saying **'blessed be Abram by God Most High,** Creator of heaven and earth'."[8] In verse twenty Melchizedek blessed the "Highest" God: "And **blessed** be God Most High, who delivered your enemies into your hand." Then, and only then, did Abraham, of his own volition, tithe to Melchizedek!

"**Then** Abram **gave** him a tenth of everything" (Gen. 14:20c, NIV). This is the same principle that men of God must do today. We must bless the people **first,** not curse them. How would you like someone to curse you? Then, do not curse others.

Balaam died for trying to curse the people of Israel. Do you realize why he tried to curse the people of God? Peter says he (Balaam) "loved the **wages** of unrighteousness" (2 Pet. 2:4). Yes! Money is one of the reasons why he tried to curse God's people. Are you Balaam? Are you pronouncing curse for "wages of unrighteousness?" Nonetheless, the truth is seen in the steps that Melchizedek followed. He did not curse, and then take by force. He blessed **before** he **received.** Glory to God!

The next point from verse six is that Melchizedek was not from the lineage of the Levitical priesthood. Yet, he received tithes from Abraham. The fact that

---

[8] See the New International Version

Melchizedek received tithe from Abraham points to the fact that our Lord Jesus is not from the Aaronic priesthood. Contrarily, Jesus is from Judah. Melchizedek is made **"like"** the Son of God. "For it is **evident** that our Lord sprang out of **Juda;** of which tribe Moses spoke nothing concerning priesthood" (Heb. 7:14, KJV).

Although Melchizedek, like our Lord is not of Aaron's lineage, he received tithe from Abraham. The Scripture then says that all of the twelve tribes tithed to Melchizedek in Abraham (Heb. 7:8-10).

The principle is this: Abraham tithed to Melchizedek, a type of Christ; thus, the church must also follow in the footstep of our father Abraham. The body of Christ must tithe to Jesus, and His priesthood. He is our "Apostle," "First Priest," Great Priest and "Chief Priest" (Heb. 3:1; 10:21). Jesus' apostles, prophets, evangelist, pastors, teachers, and saints are a part of Jesus' priesthood (Rom. 15:15-1; 1 Pet.2: 5-9). The difference is there is a **different** law.

Hebrews 7:12, KJV: For the priesthood being changed, there is made of necessity a change also of the law.

The word **change** means to translate, transferal, or transported. The priesthood was transferred from being Levitical (curses) to being like Melchizedek (life giving—Heb. 7:16). In other words, God relieved the Levitical priesthood of its duties and gave those duties to the ministers of the Church and the Church, herself.

In the process God also changed the law. The new priesthood does not curse anyone, with the exception of sorcerers (Luke 6:27-28; Acts 13:10-11). But there is also another powerful incentive for tithing to Jesus' priesthood. The law changed from being **unprofitable** to being **profitable.**

The carnal mind will think that the **"profit"** I am referring to is money. But it is not. Under the old law, when the people tithed, they were not helped spiritually. It did not make the people complete or mature in conscience (Heb. 7:18-19). Contrarily with regards to the new law, when one walks in, it produces **life.** This is because the **law** is changed.

There is another priest. His name is Jesus, the Messiah, "Who is not made (lit; birth) after the **law** of a carnal commandment, but after the **power** of an **endless life"** (Heb. 7:16). This verse is directly talking about the blessings of Jesus being High Priest. Because of our trust in Him, we have "indissolvable" life. When we tithe to Jesus we also testify (witness) of Jesus' resurrection (Heb. 7:8).

Therefore, as a person partakes of tithing, he/she also partakes of the **power of life.** Therefore, as Melchizedek blessed Abraham with life (bread and wine), before he tithed; so likewise, men of God should bless the people first. **The ministers should tell the church of the blessings of life in tithing,** and not curse them if they do not tithe. In fact, no man can curse what God has blessed (Num. 23:20, Gen. 9:1 w/Gen 9:25). The law of the Melchizedek priesthood is spiritually and naturally profitable, stronger, better, and indestructible! The law of curse is opposite (Heb. 7:18-19). In closing this chapter, I would like to take a look at one of Jesus' opinions on tithing.

*Matthew 23:23-24, KJV: Woe unto you, scribes and Pharisees, hypocrites! For you pay tithe of mint, anise, and cumin, and have omitted the weightier matters of the law, judgment, mercy, and faith: these ought you to have done, and **not leave the other [tithe] undone.** You blind guides, which strain at a gnat, and swallow a camel.*

Jesus called the Pharisees hypocrites. A hypocrite was an actor who wore a mask. Therefore, what is on the face of the mask is not the face underneath the mask. Thus, on the surface, the Pharisees seemed right because they were tithing. But beneath the tithing, they were merciless, faithless, and without justice. This hypocritical act negated their tithe.

This is the way some men of God are today. They curse God's people without **"mercy"** to get tithes. Because of their lack of **"faith,"** they use force to collect tithes. This is because there is a lack of **"judgment" or justice** among some men of God. Therefore, they become blind to the weightier matters. My advice to men of God is that with regards to the principle of tithing, be careful to also tithe mercy, faith, and justice towards God and His people. Jesus says, the Pharisees were supposed to tithe. Yet, they are not supposed to forget the weightier matter of the law. He then called them blind guides. They make a big deal out of the **gnats** (tithes). But they overlooked the **camels** (heavy matters of faith, mercy, justice, etcetera).

*Micah 8:8, KJV: He hath shewed thee, O man, what is good; and what doth the LORD require of thee, but to **do justly,** and to **love mercy,** and to **walk humbly with thy God**?*

Do not be a blind modern-day Pharisees. Thus, falling into the same ditch (compare Luke 6:39). Tithing is important to the Church of our Lord Jesus Christ, except, the priests (Church leaders) are **not** supposed to **demand** tithes. They are supposed to receive them from the people, as they give willingly. Remember, it is also the Church's duty to tithe, as grace flows from God's ministers.

Ox Principle

*Proverbs 14:4, NIV: Where there are no **oxen**, the manger is empty, but from the strength of an ox comes an abundance of harvest.*

The **ox** is the one who supplies the harvest for the manger. If the ox does not plow, then no seed can be properly sown. This truth has a spiritual significance. The "manger" can be symbolic of the Church. The "harvest" can represent the harvest of the word (seed) being planted in the saints. Harvest also symbolizes people being harvested into the kingdom of God (i.e., salvation, John 4).

Therefore, if there is no **ox** to plow then, there will be no seed planted in the believer's life. It also follows that if there is no ox, then "the manger (Church) is empty" (Compare Rom. 10:14). But "the **strength** of an ox" will bring in an abundance of saved souls. The ox needs "strength" to plow.

An ox gets some of his strength from eating (Compare Eccl. 10:17). If provision for the ox is not supplied, the ox may be hindered from plowing. The ox is then an important part of the operation of sowing and reaping. But who is the ox?

*1 Corinthians 9:9-10, NIV: [9]For it is written in the Law of Moses: "Do not **muzzle** an **ox** while it is treading out the grain." Is it about oxen that God is concerned?*

*[10]Surely he says this for **us [ministers]**, doesn't he? Yes, **this was written for us**, because when the plowman plows and the thresher threshes, they ought to do so in the hope of sharing in the harvest.*

In the verses above Paul identifies the **"ox."** He calls the ox ministers of the gospel (1 Cor. 9:5-6). The apostle says that God wrote this "ox principle" in Deut. 25:4 for the ministers of the gospel. Paul says the ox is not supposed to be **muzzled.**

A muzzle is an apparatus that prevent an animal from eating, drinking, biting, etcetera. Therefore, Paul is saying, do no prevent a man of God from partaking of the benefits necessary to maintain strength. Paul calls these benefits food, drink, expenses, grapes, and milk (1 Cor. 9:4-7). There is a catch. A minister must qualify to partake of the material harvest from the flock.

The ox is not supposed to be muzzled **"while** it is treading out the grain." A man of God may share in the material harvest (money) of the people "while it [minister] is treading (working) out the grain [word of God]" (Compare Acts 6:2-4). This also means that if a preacher is lazy, he is not supposed to live off the gospel. Do you see it? If the preacher is only eating (Phil. 3:19), and not fighting (1 Cor. 9:7); he is lazy. That preacher is not supposed to share in the Church's money.

Philippians 3:19 teach that the lazy preachers' God is their bellies. This has several meanings, one of which is that they have big bellies from eating so much and not treading out the grain (working). It is ok for a person to eat when he/she works (2 Thes. 3:10).

"Treading" (1 Cor. 9:9) demonstrates work. In calculus, I learned that work is defined as **force** multiplied by **distance.** There are a lot of preachers who do not apply their hearts **forcefully** to the work of God. The ox applies force to the plow he is pulling. The ox must also go the **"distance"** of the field to complete its task.

A man of God who does not go the **"distance"** necessary to hear from God should not get an offering. As a man of God, have you ever worked all through the night laboring in prayer and study? If the answer is no, try it. You will feel worthy of the pay you receive for your labor.

Paul says that it is only those who are "treading out the grain" who should partake of the people's material harvests. Therefore, a man of God who applies force (as graced) and goes the distance (as graced) necessary in the work of the Lord should be taken care of. It is the church's **duty** to supply material harvest to the worker, especially if the man of God is supplying correct spiritual food to the flock of God.

1 Corinthians 9:11-12, NIV: [11]*If we have sown* **spiritual seed** *among you, is it too much if we reap a* **material** *harvest from you?* [12] *If others have this right of support from you, shouldn't we have it the more?*

The other requirement for the man of God's needs being met is that he must be supplying **spiritual seed** to the people. "Spiritual seed" is the rich word of God. Yet, there are some preachers who give **carnal seeds.** The carnal seeds are teachings or doctrines that are lifeless born out of division, strife, envy, and so on. Yet, these carnal preachers are the one who demand the most support. It is only those who supply **things from the Spirit (spiritual seeds)** who are supposed to partake of financial support.

The spiritual (incorruptible) seed is the Word of God or the gospel that gives life (1 Pet. 1:12). The Word (seed) is the gospel of our salvation (deliverance) from sin (see Eph. 1:13). Ministers who are supplying the good seed (healthy doctrine) are supposed to receive "support" from the Church. Some believers are willing to support nonlocal ministers, but they are not willing to support their local minister.

In the words of Paul, "If others have this right of support from you [believers], shouldn't we [Paul and resident ministers] have it the more?" Why should Paul or a resident leader "have it [support] the more?" The reason is because the resident leader is the one who is there for the saint personally.

The Corinthian Church was the fruit of Paul (1 Cor. 9:1, NIV). He was their first resident minister. Yet others were getting financial benefits from the Church at Corinth while Paul was not. To make matters worse, these out-of-town ministers were causing division (1 Cor. 1:11-12, NIV).

In fact, some were building (teaching) wrong things on what Paul had built. Paul later called some of them false apostles and ministers, of Satan (2 Cor. 11:13-15). They were planting wrong seed on "God's field" (1 Cor. 3:9, NIV). Therefore, they were not qualified to partake of the material goods of the Church.

The Local church (people, not a building) should not muzzle the ox of that assembly. The first place the money of any saints should go is to the shepherd of that local assembly. It is the overseer of the local assembly who is like a father to that local body. Paul says: "Even though you have ten thousand guardians in Christ, you do not have many **fathers,** for in Christ Jesus I became your father through the gospel" (1 Cor. 9:15).

Paul is a **"father"** in the sense of how he treats the saints. A father comforts, urges, and encourages his children (1Thes. 2:11-12, NIV). Paul does not mean that he is the ultimate Source (Father) of the saints. The only Ultimate Source or Father of the saints is God.

Yet, Paul did birth them through the gospel (Compare Gal. 4:19). He was a father to them—an apostolic father. Therefore, a man of God who comforts, urges, and encourages the saints to live right in sincerity is deserving of material blessings from the saints. In fact, they are the man of God's wages.

1 Timothy 5:17-18, NIV: [17]*The elders who direct the affairs of the church well are worthy of double honor, especially those whose* ***work*** *is preaching and teaching.* [18]*For the Scripture says, "Do not muzzle the ox while it is treading the grain," and "The worker* ***deserves*** *his* ***wages."***

Paul called preaching and teaching **"work."** Remember, work can be defined as force multiplied by distance. It takes force to direct church affairs. In fact, a minister has more to deal with than a regular laborer. There are supernatural forces that men of

God fight against every day. Especially those who do it right!

There was a time in Paul's life when he was "harassed at every turn — conflicts on the **outside,** fears **within**" (2 Cor. 7:5, NIV). This beloved is warfare that is translated as work. It takes force to resist the conflicts of this age. This is true, especially for those who "direct church affairs" — especially for those who are on the "cutting edge" **directing the Church.**

The men of God who are working preaching and teaching are "worthy of double honor (lit., double money-paid)." The double honor includes their pay. In the words of the apostle, "The worker **deserves** his **wages.**" For those who do not pay the workers' wages, they are muzzling the ox who is feeding the flock. Allow me to give you an illustration.

One Sunday morning I posed a question to the local assembly. I asked, "Who is the person that is responsible to pay the employee?" They responded by saying, the owner or the manager.

I then said, this means if a servant works for a person, it is the person's responsibility to pay the worker (servant). Note: I know that God is the Owner. It is also God's responsibility to provide for the laborer. But do not forget, God makes his payment through His people.

Therefore, I said to the people, "If I, as a man of God, labor in the gospel for them, say, for example, until 5:00AM in the morning, it is also the Church's responsibility to pay me for those hours." Why? I am **serving** them in the work of the gospel. **Remember, when you "give" to a man of God he is not getting a handout. It is his pay. He deserves his wages.** In fact, God, Himself, said the wages received for working for Jesus is also the men of God's inheritance (Numbers 18:24-32).

In the words of Paul, our **work** is "preaching" and "teaching" the gospel of Jesus Christ. However, if I was a lazy preacher who did not have excellent work ethics, then they could be freed from that duty. This is the principle that Paul was trying to get across: it is those who "labor" or those who are "treading out the grain" who should not be muzzled.

However, in these days, it is the lazy, untrustworthy preachers who are sometimes paid the most (or should I say, they mercilessly extract their hire); while some of those who are sincere and hardworking are being muzzled. The Corinthians muzzled Paul. There were times when he had to **rob** other churches to serve (work for) the Corinthians (2

Cor. 11:8), while they were allowing themselves to be extorted by prestigious false apostles. It was the Corinthians responsibility to support Paul, however, others preaching a "different gospel" were partaking of this benefit. The point is this: it is the resident assembly's responsibility to support (pay) the overseer of that ministry, especially the one who founded the work.

Abraham was willing of himself to pay Melchizedek. He gave Melchizedek the tithe "from-all" and the spoils of war. In fact, it was Abraham and all the twelve tribes in him who tithed to Melchizedek (Heb. 7:9). "All" the saints must tithe to the priesthood of Jesus.

"Abraham gave him [Melchizedek] a tenth of **everything**" (Heb. 7:2). Again, Abraham tithed from the spoils on hand and "from-all." This means a tenth of what a person has on hand, after taxes.

In the words of Jesus, "Give [taxes] to Caesar [government] what is Caesar's, and to **God (Jesus and his priesthood) what is God's [His tithe]**" (Mat. 22:21). This is the pay God's priesthood is supposed to receive. It takes money to run a kingdom. We are of the kingdom of God.

The worldly government has public servants. These public servants (governors, senators, etcetera) "direct the affairs" of the government. Likewise, the public servants (ministers of the gospel) "direct the affairs of King Jesus' Church. Therefore, "the worker deserves his wages." This is a debt for those who receive spiritual food from their teacher; except, ministers of the New Testament does not demand or aggressively take money from God's people.

*Roman 15:27, NIV: They [Macedonians] were pleased to do it, and indeed they owe it to them. For if the Gentiles have **shared** in the Jews' **spiritual** blessings, they **owed** it to the Jews to share with them their material blessings.*

This verse is loaded with principles. The primary one has to do with giving and receiving to the poor Saints. The Macedonians were willing to send the Jews some money. This was very fitting for them to do. In fact, they (we) **"owe"** the Jews (when in need) this blessing.

The reason was that the Macedonians received salvation through a Jew (natural and spiritual Jew). His name is Jesus. This benefit for the Macedonians was a "spiritual blessing." This blessing is of the highest order. Therefore, it was the Macedonians' **duty** to give in return for the spiritual blessing.

A principle is this: A man of God gives **spiritual blessing** to the Church. It follows that the Church should reciprocate this blessing. Paul uses a stronger word. He says material blessing is **"owed"** to the giver of spiritual blessings. The King James Version says it is the **"duty"** of the recipient of spiritual blessings to give **"carnal"** blessings. Paul calls money carnal (Rom. 15:27, KJV; 1 Cor. 9:11, KJV). "If we have sown unto you spiritual things, is it a great thing if we shall reap your carnal things?"

There are two reasons why money may be considered carnal. Paul could have used this to show how **vain** it is for men of God to pursue carnality so viciously. He could also be pointing out how foolish it is for people to be "stingy" with something that is materialistic.

The Church should not make a big deal over carnal money. This is because: "You cannot serve **both** God and Money" (Mat. 6:24c, NIV). The Church must choose to let money serve the Church. Do not let the Church serve money.

The man of God should not curse those who do not give properly. It follows that the believers should not muzzle the ox (preachers). The man of God should bless the body, and the Church should pay the true ministers of the gospel.

In conclusion, the ox (burden bearer) is not supposed to be starved financially. It is by the intercession (plowing) of the ox that the manger (the Church) is filled. The ministry is work. Thus, there is energy expelled as a man of God labors in the gospel. The Church should be dutiful to pay the laborer. The good thing about this principle—God has developed a system to supply his men and the Church with the necessary funds. It is called **tithing.** Tithing existed before the Law. Therefore, tithing is a grace principle.

Tenth of All

Hebrews 7:2a, KJV: *To whom [Melchizedek] also Abraham gave a **tenth** part of **all***

Hebrews 7:2b, NIV: *And Abraham gave a **tenth** of everything.*

Hebrews 7:4, NIV: *Just think how great he was: Even the patriarch Abraham gave him **a tenth of the plunder!***

Abraham gave a **tenth of all** to Melchizedek. However, the "tenth of all" means "a tenth of [all] the spoils" of the war Abraham just won. This giving of the tenth of all happened before the Law of Moses was established. This means that tithing was practiced before the law. Thus, it is lawful to tithe to Jesus [Melchizedek] as believers. Paul says we are of the faith of Abraham (Rom. 4:16, NIV).

This faith includes the faith that Abraham demonstrated towards Melchizedek: the faith to tithe to the King of righteousness. Melchizedek is a type of Jesus. Jesus was made a priest forever after the rank of Melchizedek (Heb. 7:17).

Therefore, because we believe in Jesus, we must demonstrate this by deeds. These deeds include tithing. "Faith by itself, if not accompanied by **action**, is dead" (James 2:17, NIV). James also teaches that a believer's faith can be seen by what the believer does (James 2:18, NIV).

As we tithe to Jesus, we demonstrate our faith in Him as the High Priest. The tithe to Jesus also witnesses of His resurrection. Yet, there are also some who say that Jesus did not teach that the Church should tithe. This is not true. He did not over emphasize tithe. However, he did sanction it.

Matthew 23:23, NIV: *"Woe to you, teachers of the law and Pharisees, you hypocrites! You give a **tenth** of your **spices**--mint, dill, and cumin. But you have neglected the more important matters of the law--justice, mercy, and faithfulness. You should have practiced the latter, **without neglecting the former.***

Jesus sanctioned tithing. The problem was the leaders of the Jews were only concentrating on one thing, the tithe of substance. The same thing is happening today. Men of God talk about tithe every Church meeting. They take two (2) hours to raise offerings. However, they only spend ten (10) minutes on faith, mercy, and justice. Yet this does not negate the truth that all believers should tithe.

Jesus says practice mercy, faith, and justice **"without neglecting the former [tithes]".** The tithe of **"spices"** is money in our days. Yet this does not mean that people cannot give perishable goods to the priests of the Melchizedek order. The point is this — the Church should not "neglect" the duty of tithing. Jesus sanctioned tithing.

There is also another example of tithing before the Law of Moses. This is seen in Jacob's promise to God. This happened more than four hundred years before Moses.

Jacob was on his way to Haran. "When he reached a certain place, he stopped for the night because the sun was set" (Gen. 28:11, NIV). Jacob laid down to sleep. "He had a dream in which he saw a stairway resting on the earth, with its top (or head — Christ) reaching to heaven, and the angels of God were ascending and descending on it" (Gen. 28:12, NIV).

God also gave Jacob a message in the dream he had. When Jacob awoke, he declared, "Surely the Lord is in this **place**" (Gen. 28:16). He also said, "How **awesome** is this **place**" (Gen. 28:17, NIV). This **awesome place** is the **house of God** and the gate of heaven (Gen. 28:17, NIV). All these statements are important.

The house of God (Bethel)[9] is the Church. The Church is the "gate of heaven". Jesus through His

---

[9] Bethel is transliterated as "house of God," and the Church is called the house of God (see Gen 28:18 with Heb. 3:6).

Church is the "gate" by which people enter into heaven (John 10, Eph. 2:6). The house of God [Church] is supposed to be an awesome place.

The presence of God is supposed to be so powerful at Church meetings, the people should say, "this is an awesome place." The Church should be so awesome that people, like Jacob, should make a covenant to tithe to God. This is what Jacob did:

Genesis 28:20-22, NIV: *[20]Then Jacob made a vow, saying, "If God will be with me and will watch over me on this journey I am taking and will give me food to eat and clothes to wear [21]so that I return safely to my father's house, then the LORD will be my God [22]and this stone that I have set up as a pillar will be God's house, and of all that you give me I will give you a tenth."*

There is a lot in this text. Jacob made a covenant to **give** tithe after God spoke to him. He called the place the house of God. It is our responsibility to tithe to the house of God (Church) once we meet God in the face of Jesus (2 Cor. 4:6). Jacob said he would tithe. This was **before** any law was given.

Jacob was elected of God from the womb (Rom. 9:10-13). Likewise, the church was selected in God (Eph. 1). It follows that as Jacob tithed, the church must also tithe.

He, along with Abraham his father, is our example. In fact, one of Jacob's children (Levi) tithed in Abraham, "because when Melchizedek met Abraham, **Levi** was still in the body of his ancestor [Abraham]" (Heb. 7:10).

If Levi was in Abraham's body, then Jacob was also in Abraham's body. This is because Jacob is Levi's father. Therefore, Jacob also tithed to Melchizedek. We [the Church] were also in the body of our father Abraham, being called his "seed" [Christ] (Gal. 3:8; Gal. 3:29; Rom. 4:11).

Galatians 3:8, NIV: The Scripture foresaw that God would justify the Gentiles by faith and announced the gospel in advance to Abraham: "All nations will be blessed through you."

Galatians 3:29, NIV: If you belong to Christ, then are you Abraham's seed, and heirs according to the promise.

Romans 4:11 (last part), NIV: So then, he [Abraham] is the father of all who believe but have not been circumcised, in order that righteousness might be credited to them.

The Church is **"Abraham's seed"** through faith in Jesus. **We,** his **spiritual** seed, were also **in** Abraham when he met Melchizedek. Abraham **"is the father of all who believe"**. Do you see it now? Thus, in the spirit through our faith in Jesus (the true Melchizedek), "we" tithed in Abraham.

This means as followers of Jesus, we must presently give Him our tithe. This is done by faith as our father Abraham did when he met Melchizedek. Today, we see Melchizedek in the form of Jesus (Heb. 7:17-22).

Now do not be over wise and say, "Abraham tithed for us, so we do not have to pay tithe". The Book says, "One might even say that Levi, who collects the tenth, **paid** the tenth through Abraham" (Heb. 7:9). There are two principles in this verse. I will only cover one.

Levi did tithe in Abraham. However, even though Levi tithed through Abraham, Levi still **received** tithe from the people. It follows that even though we (the Church) tithed through Jesus (the greater Abraham), the Melchizedek priesthood (ministers) should still receive tithe from the Church.

Abraham tithe from "everything" to also include, but not limited to, a tenth of "all" of the spoils. The tithe (tenth) is supposed to be out of everything in one's accumulations. That is, the tenth is supposed to be "from-whole" of his accumulation as exemplified by Abraham after his conquest of the kings.

Abraham gave a tenth of the plunder that were on hand; and he also gave to Melchizedek a tenth "from all-whole" of his accumulation.[10] With that said, a person may choose not to pay tithe on the taxes[11] taken out of their income, until they receive a tax return.

*2 Corinthians 8:12, NIV: For if the willingness is there, the gift is acceptable **according to what one has,** not according to what he does not have.*

Paul exemplified the principle of giving *"according to what one has, not according to what he does not have."* This means if a person <u>nets</u> $100.00 per week **after** taxes, then, the tithe of this amount is one hundred dollars multiplied by ten percent ($100 x 0.10). This equals $10.00 or, ten percent (10%) of the $100.00.

This is simple. We should not complicate the matter. The tithe is a tenth of "what one has." This is the tenth of "everything" or "all" that is in one's possession. **With that said, if someone chooses to tithe off his/her gross income, this is also acceptable (2 Cor. 9:7).** In addition, the priests are also to tithe of everything they receive. In other words, preachers are also to give, and if necessary,

---

[10] Genesis 14:20, Genesis 14:23 and Hebrews 7:2, Hebrews 7:4

[11] Note: Some may prefer to tithe from the gross <u>in lieu</u> of the net (2 Cor. 9:7).

they are also to give more than a tenth (Acts 20:33-35).

In Malachi, God taught us that it was the **whole nation** of Israel who was robbing God (Mal. 3: 8-10). In chapter one of this volume, I demonstrated how the priests were included in this group. In fact, God called the whole nation (this includes priests) **robbers.** The next question is, how did the priests (preachers) **rob** God? They were also robbing God of tithes. The priests are supposed to tithe to the high priest and the storehouse. First, I will look at the tithe to the storehouse.

Malachi 3:10, NIV: Bring the whole tithe into the *storehouse, that there may be food in my house.*

Preachers have used the verse cited above to demand money from the saints. However, they miss a key point. They are supposed to tithe to the storehouse, **too.** In the New Testament, Paul not only received giving from the Church (Philippians 4:14-19); Paul also gave back to the house of God, the people of the living God (Acts 20:33-35)

With that said, Nehemiah also beautifully displayed how the ministers of God are supposed to tithe. This is what is said in Nehemiah 10:38, after the temple was **rebuilt.**

*Nehemiah 10:38, NIV: A priest descended from Aaron is to accompany the Levites when they receive the tithes, and the Levites are to bring a tenth of the tithes up to the **house of our God,** to the storerooms of the treasury.*

From this, the reader can understand why God made the whole nation responsible for robbing God. The preachers were also stealing God's tithe. They were not taking a tenth of the tithe and putting it into the "treasury" for the benefit of others.

Note: This principle concerning storing up in a treasury for the benefit of others, in context to the grace of giving, is only true if there is a surplus; and in addition, tithing is no longer to an institutional building, but to a God ordained person in the ministry (1 Corinthians 9:13-14).

Also, One might say why does God need money (tenth of the tithe) in His storehouse? This is simple. There may come a day when things get challenging and if a ministry had the capacity to save, help can be available from that savings. Joseph is an example of this principle when he saved twenty percent (20%) of Pharaoh's income in the years of plenty.

Jesus also said, "Haven't you read what David did when he and his companions were **hungry?** He entered the **house** of God and ate the consecrated bread — which was not lawful for them to do, but only for the priest" (Matt. 12:3-4, NIV). There were some things that were unlawful to do (2 Cor. 12:4). However, like David, in time of emergency or **necessity**, everything "constructive" will be lawful (1 Cor. 10:23, NIV).

It was "constructive" for David to eat because of his destiny. This truth makes it "lawful" for the priest to help him with God's bread. In fact, it was the bread of God's **presence**.

So likewise, it will be for "constructive" purposes the Church is supposed to have a storehouse (emergency funds) for those in the body, if there is a surplus. The Church, like David, is destined for rulership in the earth (Rom. 5:17). The Church must be prepared to sustain the saints by provisions reserved in the storehouses in times of emergencies.

God makes it right for the priest (preachers) to tithe from the tenth they receive. This tenth of the tithe is supposed to be **stored up** for emergencies (compare the fifth part of Joseph stored up in advance of the great famine). In the words of the prophet Malachi, "that there may be **food** in my house". At one point in David's life, there was no "ordinary bread" (food) for David and his men (1 Sam. 21:4). Therefore, the priest had to use consecrated bread to feed David and his men (1 Sam. 21:6).

It is safe to say, there was no food in the storehouse, because the priest had to use **old** bread (1 Sam. 21:6). New bread is supposed to be placed every day. The priest also said, "I don't have **any** ordinary bread on hand" (1 Sam. 21:4). This is no surprise because Saul (type of unspiritual rulers) was in charge. However, if there were food in God's house, David and his men could have eaten properly.

This is one of the reasons why God was so "hard" on the priests in Malachi. They were not tithing to God from the tenth they received. Therefore, there was no food in the storehouse and treasury of God to be able to help other. The next thing that the priests were to practice was that they should tithed to the high priest.

Jesus is our High Priest (Heb. 3:1). Therefore, when the preachers do not tithe to the High Priest, Jesus, they are robbing God. In other words, a tenth of the tithe received should go to Jesus. Let us take a look at the scripture to see how the High Priest is supposed to be treated with regards to tithing.

*Numbers 18:26, NIV: "Speak to the **Levites** and say to them: 'When you receive from the Israelites the **tithe** I give you as **your** inheritance, you must present a tenth of that tithe as **the Lord's offering**".*

The Levites can point to two groups. The Levites were also priests. Therefore, the first group of Levites is the **priesthood** of believers: "But you are a chosen people, a royal **priesthood**" (1 Pet. 2:9).

This shows us that all believers should "present a tenth of that tithe as the Lord's offering." Yet there is a stronger point in the verse above. The **Levites** point to all the ministers of the gospel (1 Corinthians 9:13-14). The tithe the ministers receive from the "Israelites" (Church) is **their "inheritance"**.

Yes, **all the tithes** that come into a local assembly (not an institutional building, but a body of believers) are the **inheritance** of the recognized leadership of that assembly. There are a lot of saints who are disrespectful to their Levites (ministers).

They get angry when men of God use the inheritance (i.e., money received) God gave the ministers of the gospel. This should not be. The next note is that "the Lord's offering" is really the high priest's. That is, God gave His offering to Aaron. Aaron is a type of Jesus Christ (Heb. 5:4-5).

*Numbers 18:28, NIV: In this way you [Levites] also will present an offering to the Lord from all the tithes you receive from the Israelites. From these tithe you must give the **Lord's portion** to Aaron the priest.*

Aaron (Jesus) is supposed to get the **Lord's portion.** In verse twenty-eight of the same chapter the Lord's portion is called "the **best** and **holiest** part of everything given to you" (Num. 18:29, NIV). The best belongs to Jesus our High Priest. Jesus has the "preeminence" in all things. Therefore, a tenth of everything should be given to the Melchizedek priesthood of Jesus.

The purpose for this is to have meat in God's storehouse, meat for those serving as ministers in the gospel of Jesus Christ. If there are no tithes from the people, then, there will not be any tithes for the priests. It follows that there will be no tithes for the high priest, Jesus. Thus, there also will not be any meat (emergency savings) in God House for those ministries who have the capacity to save.

The Aaronic priesthood also points to Jesus Christ and the **many** apostolic and prophetic ministries in the body of Christ: "And in the Church God has appointed **first** apostles, **second** prophets" (1 Cor. 12:28). The apostle and prophets, along with Jesus, are the **foundations** of the Church (Eph. 2:20, Rom. 15:16).

The Aaronic priesthood also points to Jesus and the entire ministry corps (apostles, prophets, teachers, evangelist, and pastors, helps, governments, etcetera (Eph. 4:11, 1 Cor. 12). There is a priesthood of elders in the body of Christ. The scripture says that there are "twenty-four elders" before the throne of God.

Revelation 4:4, NIV: Surrounding the throne were ***twenty-four elders.*** *They were dressed in white and had crowns of gold on their heads.*

The word elder is the Greek word **"presbuteros."** As a noun, the word means **senior.** This is the word that leaders use to call themselves "Senior Pastors". This is also the word used for "elders" in the Church. **"Presbuteros"** is transliterated "presbyter." A "presbyter" or presbyters are the leaders of the Church. The next point is this:

There were **twenty-four** of them (elders) before the throne of God. In 1 Chronicles 24, there were **twenty-four (24) high priests** designated to serve in the temple David and Solomon established. From this we learn that **"24"** is the number for the priesthood.

Therefore, in the book of Revelation, the "twenty-four elders" are the corporate priests of the Church. These priests are the sons of **The High Priest — Jesus** (Heb. 3:1), in the same manner as the "24" high priests in I Chronicles 24 were "sons of Aaron" (1 Chron. 24:1; 19).

As I stated above, Aaron is a type of Christ (Heb. 5:4-5). It follows that Aaron's sons are a type of the ministers of Christ. Aaron's sons continued the priesthood duties. We do the same, except our priesthood follows the Melchizedek order (Heb. 7). The "invited" ministers function as a **corporate** high priest (see also Hebrews 9 and Hebrews 10).

Therefore, **corporately** they are a type of Aaron. It should not be an awkward thing for the Church to give "the best and holiest part of everything" they earn to the ministers of the gospel. The tenth was "wages for your [ministers] work at the Tent of Meeting [Church]" (Num. 18:31).

Ministering in the temple was a heavy responsibility for the priests. Likewise, ministering to the temple (the Church—Eph. 2:19-22) is a tedious task (2 Cor. 11:28). This is especially true if the men of God do it the right way. Therefore, tithe should be given. It was death to those Levites who did not tithe to the high priest

*Numbers 18:32, NIV: By presenting the best part of it you will not be **guilty** in this matter; then you will not defile the holy offerings of the Israelites, **and you will not die.***

When a minister gives tithes to Jesus our High Priest then, he will not feel **"guilty."** Guilt comes when saints do not tithe. Also, when the ministers tithe from the tenth they received, the "holy offerings" **will not** be defiled. But if the tenth is not given, then, the offering is **defiled,** and the priest may **die.** It also follows that when saints do not tithe to the local leaders any other offering are considered **defiled.** There will also be a guilt that may lead to death.[12] Beloved, this is serious.

There was a husband and wife who decided to keep back a part of the money they had received from a transaction. They lied to the man of God (an apostle) concerning the amount they had received. Consequently, they gave **less** than what was proper. The Apostle Peter (a priest of Jesus) confronted them. They had actually lied to the Holy Spirit. Their penalty for **lying** and not giving **honestly** was **death.** This incident happened in the Church (Acts 5:1-10).

The same thing is going to happen in our days. Some could die for lying in order to keep back a portion of their offerings. Not paying the tithe may lead to death as says the "law;" yet in the New Testament, through Jesus' "grace" the Holy Spirit appears to judge for lying to the Holy Spirit in His apostles and prophets about giving and receiving for the poor

---

[12] In the New Testament death only occurred when a few people "lied" to the Holy Spirit about their giving relative to their income

saints. I reiterate this is a serious matter. Saints should not muzzle the ox that is working in the field.

It will not be profitable for the ones who hold back tithes and offerings. The Church must get a proper perspective. The man of God, except for our Lord Jesus, is one of the most important people in one's life. We carry "the gospel of **your** salvation" (Eph. 2:13).

Therefore, as the scripture teaches, it is the believers' **duty to give tithe** and **give offerings.** One should be happy to help those who are helping them. Remember it is more blessed to give than to receive.

Men of God are **happy** when they **give** the gospel to the Church without charge. The saints should also **happily** give of their substance to the man of God. Therefore, **both** are "blessed" because, they **gave. It is more blessed to give.**

Tithe-Seeing the Prince

*Genesis 14:18-20, NIV: ¹⁸Then Melchizedek … priest of God Most High, ¹⁹… blessed Abram … ²⁰…. Then Abram gave him **a tenth of everything (lit., from-tenth from-all)**.*

We are to tithe without being asked to tithe or prompted to tithe upon genuinely experiencing the Lord Jesus! Saying it another way, the Lord Jesus' disciples will tithe to the Lord Jesus and His together-priesthood, of their own volition, if they really have an encounter with the Lord Jesus!

The Scripture said let every word be established in two or three witnesses (2 Cor. 13:1). Here are three witnesses.

1. Genesis 14 (a first witness): After Abraham met Melchizedek, Melchizedek giving Abraham bread and wine (the communion of the body and blood of Jesus); and Melchizedek blessing God and Abraham; Abraham **tithe** to Melchizedek without being asked to do so. Hebrews 7:4, said that we should spectate, as in a theatre, Melchizedek's greatness and vastness which caused Abraham to tithe to him without being asked to do so. Thus, through Abraham's encounter and personal experience with the King-of-Righteousness,

priest of the Highest God, he tithes to Melchizedek.

The same is true to us, when we really experience the communion of the bread and blood of Jesus, experiencing God's blessing (Jesus our Savior) we will tithe to Jesus, our Melchizedek, without being asked to do so by preachers and/or tithe to His "together-priesthood" without man forcing us to tithe!

2. Genesis 28 (a second witness): After Jacob met the Lord Jesus (Genesis 28:12-13; John 1:51) through a dream encountering "the Lord" at the "top"(lit., head) of the ladder (a symbol of the Lord Jesus) that reached heaven, Jacob of his own volition decided to tithe to the Lord God of "all" that the Lord will give him. Again, no other human prompted Jacob to tithe. Jacob vowed to tithe out of his personal encounter with the Lord; and we are to do the same!

3. Genesis 14:20; 23 (a third witnesses): The Hebrew word for tithe is "mosher" (מעשר). A Hebrew pictograph that can be formed from this word is: after "seeing (experiencing)-the prince," we tithe "from" our "accumulations." That is, the Hebrew word for tithe is from a root word "eser" (עשר) which by definition

means accumulation, wealth, and riches, according to Strong's dictionary (Genesis 14:23).

The word "eser" (עשר) is made up the letters ayin (ע), a picture of an eye, to see, to experience, to know, and Hebrew letters that is also used for "prince"(שר), shin (ש) and resh (ר). "Mim" (מ) used as a prefix in the word for tithe "mosher" (מעשר) means "from." Hence, a Hebrew pictograph of the word "tithe" ["mosher" (מעשר)] can be interpreted as "tithing is 'from-experiencing-(the)-prince.'"

In other words, we tithe to the Lord Jesus from our accumulations He gave us, when we "experience the Prince," Jesus! We tithe without prompting by human influence. We tithe because we have met Jesus, in truth! **It is more blessed to give.**

Excel in this Grace of Giving

*2 Corinthians 8:7, NIV: But just as you excel in everything--in faith, in speech, in knowledge, in complete earnestness and in your love for us--see that you also **excel in this grace of giving.***

The "grace of giving" is something in which all Christians should excel. Most like the idea of excelling in the **other** operations of grace. Yet, it seems difficult to also excel in this grace of giving. One of the reasons could be a lack of true understanding of giving. There have been wrong conclusions based upon wrong premises. Thus, there are fallacies concerning the principle of giving.

First, a person must realize that giving is a grace. Grace means favor, among its other uses. Therefore, giving to someone is like showing him/her favor. It makes the recipient feel good **towards God** because someone cares enough to impart a gift to that person (2 Cor. 9:12-13). The Scriptures also teaches that giving money to a person is the same as "speaking well" over that person. However, there is **"Someone"** else I would like to use to demonstrate this grace of giving.

*2 Corinthians 8:9, NIV: For you know the **grace** of our Lord **Jesus** Christ, that though **he was rich,** yet for your* *sake **he became poor,** so that you through his poverty might become rich.*

This is a true definition of grace. True grace is also demonstrated when Jesus became poor that we may be made rich.[13] He left His heavenly glory and took on the form of "slave … man."

He "made himself **nothing,** taking the very nature of a servant [slave] **being made** in human (man's) likeness" (Phil. 2:7, NIV). Jesus made Himself **nothing.** This also means He became **poor.** The result of His poverty is riches for us.

"In him **we have** redemption through his blood, the forgiveness of sins, in accordance with the **riches of God's grace**" (Eph. 1:7, NIV). "We have" because **He gave** to us His **riches.** However, He became poor **for a time (approximately 33.5 years)** in the process.

First, Grace (Jesus) is a giver. Next, we learn that when a person gives, a giver can experience a deficit. This means that whenever a saint gives, he may experience a deficit for a time. Let me explain a little more. There are people who do not like to give because, when they give, for a time, they may have a lack. But we must give with understanding.

---

[13] The New Testament list at least ten (10) spiritual riches we inherit through Jesus Christ.

*Ecclesiastes 11:1, NIV: Cast your bread (money) upon the waters, for **after many days** you will find it again.*

It is **"after many days"** that a giver will receive a return. The understanding is that when a saint gives, **there may** be a period of no reaping until the appointed time of the harvest. When we give to someone, we "will find it [that which was given] again." Do you see it now? Therefore, when a believer has this understanding, he will continue to give; even though, they go through a brief period of lack. This same principle is seen in the book of Psalms.

Psalm 102:13-14, KJV: [13] *You shalt arise, and have **mercy** upon Zion: for the time to favor her, yes, the set time, is come.* [14] ***For** her servants take **pleasure** in her stones and **favor** the dust thereof.*

The Scripture says that God would "have mercy upon Zion" (the Church) — mercy being one of His riches (Eph. 2:4). Again, Zion is a place where, the Church is come to (Heb. 12:22-23). Zion is the Church (1 Pet. 2:5-6). The Psalm then says, "The **set** time **is** come" to **favor** the Church.

All these statements were made because something else happened, first. In the word of the text, **"For** her servants take pleasure in her stones." These "stones" are people. Peter calls the Church living stones (1

Pet. 2:5). "Pleasure" means "to be pleased with" and **"to satisfy a debt"** (Strong's Concordance #7521).

The phrase could read **her servants satisfy the debt of the stones**. What does this mean, brother Peart? This means that if I have one hundred dollars that I need, and you need one hundred dollars, I will give you the one hundred dollars.

Therefore, I am **satisfying your debt.** I am actually becoming poor (temporarily) that you may be rich. That is, I really do need the one hundred dollars. Yet, I am willing to go without that you may have. This, beloved, is grace giving. As a result, God will show the Church mercy and favor. Do you see it now?

This can be understood as part of the meaning when it said our Lord became poor that we may be made rich. Jesus saw a need in us. We needed salvation. He then emptied Himself, or should I say, He gave himself **for** and **to** us. In the process He became poor leaving all His heavenly riches for a short season. The result of the debt He satisfied is riches for us.

We should be willing to do the same thing. The Church should get to the place where we are willing to lack for a time (if God wills it) that others may be relieved. A Church I once attended was in desperate need of finance. There was a brother in the Church who had received a considerable sum of money. God told him to give one thousand dollars ($1,000) of that money to the church. He did not.

Two of this brother's favorite sayings were this: "If I give to others, I am **afraid I** won't have," and, "If I give to others then I will be poor." Obviously, he did not know the Scripture concerning the giving of Jesus.

In fact, as time passed, debts that this person did not know or remembered existed started appearing out of nowhere, and he could not pay the debts. The lesson is this: He did not satisfy the debt of others; therefore, God did not immediately help him with his debt. Jesus says, "Give and **it will** be given to you" (Luke 6:38).

The next principle I will cover is the foremost reason Paul wrote this principle called the "grace of giving." The truth of the matter is this verse was written on behalf of the "poor among the saints in Jerusalem" (Rom. 15:26). This is an important concept.

Today the Church targets her giving efforts to the poor, unsaved world. This is good to do. Yet, it is not necessarily right or complete. The reason is the Church is giving to the poor of this world. Yet, the poor saints in the Church are not being ministered to properly. Let me give an example before the reader misunderstands.

The body of Christ has saints who do not eat regularly, every day. There are poor believers in the Church who cannot afford to go to college, or trade school among other things. They may not be able to gain a scholarship for school, but capable of completing school, if supported.

The Church as a whole should establish a fund for "poor saints" like these. But the money is spent on the poor in the world more than the poor in the Church. Again, this does not mean that the church should not give to the poor in the world. The Church should **continue** to give to the poor in this world, with the understanding that they need to be taught the gospel of the kingdom (see my book *The Lamb*).

There was woman who anointed Jesus' body with **expensive perfume.** Jesus taught that the woman's act was preparation for His burial. The disciples complained saying, "This perfume could have been sold for a **high price** and the **money** given to the **poor**" (Mat. 26:9). Jesus replied: "The poor you will **always** have with you, but you will not always have me" (Mat. 26:11). Allow me to explain these verses in light of what I said above.

"Poor" in the Greek means "**pauper.**" One of the definitions of pauper is to be unproductive. Jesus said there would **always** be unproductive people in the world. He then said, "But you will not **always have me.**" So likewise, a poor believer in the church will not "always" be with us.

Therefore, we should put some "perfume" (expense) in the "body" of believers before their burial. That is, the Church should be willing to spend money on other poor followers of Christ to help them to be productive in life. You may help provide money for schooling now but reap a harvest of tithe and offering later.

The "right" thing about this is it will add asset to the Church. The poor believers who could not give, after gaining a skill and finding a job, can "potentially" give back more to the Church. There will always be poor people. But the poor in the church are supposed to be helped first. Did the reader know that love is measured by what we do for the poor **believers?**

*1 John 3:16-19, NIV: This is how we know what love is: Jesus Christ laid down his life for us. And we ought to lay down our lives for our **brothers**. If anyone has **material** possessions and sees his brother **in need** but has no pity on him, **how can the love of God be in him?** Dear children, let us not love with words or tongue but with*

*actions. This then is how we **know** that we belong to
the truth, and how we set our hearts at rest in his presence*

These verses are most beautiful. Our hearts can rest
in God's presence when we give to the brothers and
sisters of the Church. The verses did not say we
would have rest when we give to the poor in this
world. **Note:** I am **not** saying do not to give to the
poor in this world at all. What I am saying is, **give to
the poor saints first.** The Church has it backwards.

Paul was encouraging the Corinthian Church to do
the right thing: give to the poor saints at Jerusalem.
We should do the same. The Church as a whole
should give to the poor saints of the body of Christ,
with the understanding that the poor also needs to
be taught how to be self-sufficient in the kingdom of
God.

The leadership of the body should have good
discernment to know who a true brother is, and who
is not. Therefore, the Church will not be exploited.
Giving also creates **equality** in the body. That is, as
a person supplies to those who lack now, when the
giver lacks his needs will also be supplied.

*2 Corinthians 8:13-14, NIV: Our desire is not that
others might be relieved while you are hard pressed, but
that there might be **equality**. At the present time, your
plenty will supply what they need, so that in turn their*

plenty will supply what you need. Then there will be equality.

This is the way the Church is supposed to be. **Now, I am not advocating giving to freeloaders** (2 Thess. 3:10). Yet we should be sensitive to the need of the saints. Why? Someday you may need someone to help you. Did you know that the Scripture says that when a person is kind to the poor, he/she is lending to the Lord, and the Lord will reward the giver (see Pr. 19:17)?

Beloved, "God is not unjust; he will not forget your work and the love you have shown him **as** you have helped his people and continue to help them" (Heb. 6:10, NIV). Therefore, there will be equality. God will insure that there is a reward for those who give to the poor. But there is also a **penalty** for those who do not give to the ones in need.

2 Corinthians 8:15, NIV: As it is written: "He who gathered much did not have too much, and he who gathered little did not have too little."

This quote by Paul was taken from Exodus 16:18. In reading Exodus the reader will quickly learn that the verse has to do with "manna." Manna means **who** and **what?** The "who" is Jesus (John 6)! The "what" in the context of 2 Corinthians 8 is Jesus' money!

The people complained to Moses because there was no food. The Lord then sent them "manna" from heaven. The rule was: do not take more than necessary. There was always enough for each family. The big family had enough, and the little family had enough. Yet, there is something more to the fact that Paul used this verse while he was discussing giving **money.** Manna is equated to Money. Therefore, the wisdom of God can be seen in the study of Exodus and Corinthians together.

This is what Moses says in Exodus: "No one is to keep any [manna] until morning" (Ex. 16:19, NIV). However, some of them ignored Moses; they **kept part** of it until morning, but it was full of **maggots** and began to **smell.** Thus, Moses became angry with them (Ex. 16:20).

In context of 2 Corinthians 8, a person who has "kept a part" of his money (manna) and does not give it to those who need, it ("manna-money") becomes rotten and "smells." Maggots (nasty circumstances) will eat the money.

Yes, for the "stingy" folks, their money will "smell" and "maggot situations" will eat the money (manna). Thus, there is a judgment on those who have extra and do not give. The money (manna) that maggots ate and that smelled was only for those who **"kept a part".**

There were some believers who died, because they **"kept back part of the money for"** themselves (Acts 5:2, NIV). Note: this money that Peter and the other apostles were collecting was for the **poor** saints (Acts 4:34). Keeping back "a part" from the poor saints is serious stuff. The money kept back will become stink and full of maggots. This act will also cause death.

Death includes natural death (Acts 5:5), and spiritual death (Compare 1 Tim. 5:6, Rev. 3:1). That is, a person can be alive, yet that person can be considered dead (Rev. 3:1). A business, prayer life, ministry, relationships, and so on, may die due, in part, to the fact of withholding "a part" that belongs to those who are in need.

Paul called this "part" — "plenty" (see 2 Cor. 8:14 in the New International Version). In the King James translation, it is rendered "abundance." The Greek word means "**surplus.**" This seems to mean that that which is left over **after** bills are paid, necessities are met, and for those who can save, the surplus after savings (Deut. 28:8; 12, etcetera).

This "surplus" should be given (should the opportunity presents itself) to the saint who may have needs. If you do not have a surplus, you cannot give. But for those who do, they should be willing and ready to give. Does the reader know that giving from surplus builds a foundation for the coming age?

*1 Timothy 6:17-19, NIV: Command those who are **rich** (have plenty of surplus) in this present world not to be arrogant nor to put their hope in wealth, which is so uncertain, but to put their hope in God, who richly provides us with everything for our enjoyment. Command them to do good, to be rich in good deeds, and to be generous and **willing** to share. In this way they will lay up treasure for themselves as a firm foundation for the coming age, so that they may **take hold** of the eternal life that is truly life.*

I am about to say something unknown. Giving is part of the way that the rich (those who have surplus) "take hold of eternal life" (compare 1 Tim. 6:12). Giving out of your surplus builds a **firm** foundation for the coming age.

Do not let your money "smell" in the bank when there are **poor saints** who live on the verge of being put out of their homes every month. Do not let your surplus be **eaten** by maggots when that money can put **food** on the table of the poor saints. Do not allow money (manna) to be left over until morning, when expectation in God might die because of stinginess.

If you are rich (having plenty of surpluses) send a saint to school. Help a brother and sister in the Lord with their necessities (if needed). We are all one. We all have one Father, God. Who would let a natural family member die if he had the money to help? So likewise, the Church is a family (Eph. 3:14-15). We are members of the same body. Therefore, all things should be in common. This is what the apostles promoted in their day.

*Acts 4:32, NIV: All the believers were **one** in heart and mind. No one claimed that any of his possession was his own, but they shared **everything** they had.*

I conclude on these notes. A true believer will share out of what he/she has with the poor saints and the local assembly of God's people. The beautiful thing about this is that "With **great power** the apostles continued to testify to the resurrection of the Lord Jesus, **and much grace** was upon them all. There were no needy persons among them" (Acts 4:33-34a, NIV).

"Much grace (favor) was upon them all." This is what the writer **predicted** would happen in Psalm 102:13-14 for those who pay the debt of others. The result was God granted "great power" to the apostles. Yes, when we take care of one another, God's power will show up on the scene! In the words of Psalms, God will "show favor [grace] to her [the Church]."[14]

---

[14] Ps 102:13, KJV

Paul echoed this concerning cheerful and willing givers by saying, "And God is able to make **all grace** abound to you, so that in **all things,** having **all** that you **need,** you will abound in every good work." As it is also written, "'He has scattered abroad his gifts to the poor; his righteousness endures forever' "(1 Cor. 9:8-9). One of the ways "all grace" and "great power" will be manifested in the Church is by giving willingly to those who are in need. I encourage you to **"see that you also excel in this grace of giving"** (2 Cor. 8:7, NIV).

Other Books

Poiema, by Judith Peart
Wisdom from Above, by Judith Peart
Procreation, Understanding Sex, and Identity, by Judith Peart
100 Nevers, by Judith Peart
The Shattered and the Healing by Judith Peart
The Lamb, by Donald Peart
Jesus' Resurrection, Our Inheritance, by Donald Peart.
Sexuality, By Donald Peart
Forgiven 490, by Donald Peart w/Judith Peart!
The Days of the Seventh Angel, By Donald Peart
The Torah (The Principle) of Giving, by Donald Peart
The Time Came, by Donald Peart
The Last Hour, the First Hour, the Forty-Second Generation, by Donald Peart
Vision Real, by Donald Peart
The False Prophet, Alias, Another Beast V1, by Donald Peart
"the beast," by Donald Peart
Son of Man Prophesy Against the false prophet, by Donald Peart
The Many False Prophets (The Dragon's Tail), by Donald Peart
The Work of Lawlessness Revealed, by Donald Peart
When the Lord Made the Tempter, by Donald Peart
Examining Doctrine, Volume 1, by Donald Peart
Exousia, Your God Given Authority, by Donald Peart
The Numbers of God, by Donald Peart
The Completions of the Ages … by Donald Peart
The Revelation of Jesus Christ, by Donald Peart
Jude—Translation and Commentary, by Donald Peart
Obtaining the Better Resurrection, by Donald Peart
Manifestations from Our Lord Jesus ...by Donald and Judith Peart).
Obtaining the Better Resurrection, by Donald Peart
The New Testament, Dr. Donald Peart Exegesis
The Tree of Life, By Dr. Donald Peart
The Spirit and Power of John, the Baptist by Dr. Donald Peart
The Shattered and the Healing by Judith Peart
Is She Married to a Husband? by Donald Peart
The Ugliest Man God Made by Donald Peart
Does Answering the Call of God Impact Your Children? by Donald Peart
Victory Out-of-the Beast-the Harvest of the Earth by Donald Peart
The Order of Melchizedek by Donald Peart
Ezekiel-the House-the City-the Land (Interpreting the Patterns) by Donald Peart
Butter and Honey, Understanding how to Chose the Good and Refuse the Evil, by Donald Peart

Contact Information:

Crown of Glory Ministries
P.O. Box 1041 Randallstown, MD 21133
donaldpeart7@gmail.com

About the Author:

Donald Peart is married to Judith Peart since 1986; and they believe that Jesus is the Christ, the Son of the living God; and they teach the gospel of God's kingdom centered on Jesus Christ and His ecclesia. They are the parents of six children, including their daughter-in-law. They have founded and currently oversee Crown of Glory Ministries in Randallstown, Maryland. Donald and his wife have written over thirty-seven books; and their ministry has distributed their book to at least 29 States in the USA and 21 countries. In his early years of ministry, the Lord Jesus graced Donald to have studied the Word of God extensively and in depth (sometimes studying for over 8 hours per day for many years). The Lord Jesus has graced Donald to earn an Associate of Arts degree in Pre-Engineering, a Bachelor of Science degree in Civil Engineering, a Master of Divinity, a Master of Science in Construction Management, and a Doctorate in Theology.

www.ingramcontent.com/pod-product-compliance
Lightning Source LLC
Chambersburg PA
CBHW060413050426
42449CB00009B/1964